W9-DIS-969

NBA
Superstars

by James Buckley, Jr.

SCHOLASTIC INC.

New York   Toronto   London   Auckland   Sydney
Mexico City   New Delhi   Hong Kong   Buenos Aires

To Conor, another kind of superstar!

All photos courtesy of NBAE/Getty Images, unless otherwise noted.
Cover: (Carter), 26: Nathaniel S. Butler. Cover (Kidd), 15, 16, 21, 23, 24: Noren Trotman.
Cover (Bryant), 10, 11, 41: Robert Mora. Cover (McGrady), 34: Andy Hayt. 4, 6: Gary Dineen.
5: Joe Murphy. 7: Jonathan Daniel. 8, 9, 30: Andrew D. Bernstein. 12, 14: Ron Turenne. 13: Sam
Forencich. 17: Garrett W. Ellwood. 18, 22, 37: Jesse Garrabrant. 19, 40: David Sherman.
27, 28: Fernando Medina. 29: Paul Chapman. 31, 38, 39: Rocky Widner. 32, 33, 36: Glenn
James. 35: Colin Fisher-Jones. 43: Gary Dineen/NBA Photos. 44 (Bryant):
Andrew D. Bernstein/NBA Photos. 44 (Carter): Ron Turenne/NBA Photos. 45 (Garnett): David
Sherman/NBA Photos. 45 (Kidd): Sandy Tenuto/NBA Entertainment. 46 (McGrady): Fernando
Medina/NBA Photos. 47 (Nowitzki): Layne Murdoch/NBA Entertainment.
47 (Pierce): Derek Fowles/NBA Photos. 48: Rocky Widner/NBA Photos.

If you purchased this book without a cover, you should be aware that this book is stolen
property. It was reported as "unsold or destroyed" to the publisher, and neither the
author nor the publisher has received any payment for this "stripped book."

No part of this publication may be reproduced in whole or in part, or stored in a retrieval
system, or transmitted in any form or by any means, electronic, mechanical, photocopying,
recording, or otherwise, without written permission of the publisher.
For information regarding permission, write to Scholastic Inc.,
Attention: Permissions Department, 557 Broadway, New York, NY 10012.

The NBA and individual NBA member team identifications, photographs, and other content
used on or in this publication are trademarks, copyrighted designs, and other forms of
intellectual property of NBA Properties, Inc., and the respective NBA member teams and
may not be used, in whole or in part, without the prior written consent of
NBA Properties, Inc. All rights reserved.

ISBN 0-439-44302-4

Copyright © 2002 by NBA Properties, Inc.
All rights reserved. Published by Scholastic Inc.

SCHOLASTIC and associated logos are trademarks
and/or registered trademarks of Scholastic Inc.

12 11 10 9 8 7 6 5 4 3 2 1   2 3 4 5 6 7/0

Printed in the U.S.A.
First Scholastic printing, September 2002
Book Design: Louise Bova

Contents

Ray Allen

The Sweet Shooter

"In order to be a good shooter, it's important to practice 'game shots.' What I mean by this is, there are certain shot opportunities you know you'll receive in games and when you do, you have to be ready."
— Ray Allen

Sweet-shooting Ray Allen knows all about hitting big "game" shots. The Milwaukee Bucks' shooting guard has one of the best jump shots in the league. He combines a great shooting touch with amazing quickness and is one of the NBA's most complete players.

Opponents know that when Ray aims for the basket, they're in trouble. Ray has a career average of more than 19 points per game.

Want strong bones? got milk?

He has often been among the league's top 20 in scoring. And he's not just making little jumpers. He can nail shots from long range, too. In 2001, he won the 1 800 CALL ATT Shootout. This event is held at the All-Star Game and features the league's best three-point artists.

Ray is even a great shooter when he's standing still. He has made more than 87 percent of his career free throws. He is one of the NBA's best free throw shooters!

The Bucks are very glad he makes all those pretty shots for them. Since early in his career, Ray has been at or near the top of the team's scoring stats. But that's not the only way he has helped make the Bucks a top team. Ray regularly pulls down more than four rebounds per game. And as the shooting guard, he is often matched up on defense against the opponent's best player.

The former University of Connecticut star is one of the NBA's most dependable players. He has played in nearly every game for the Bucks since joining the team in

1996. That means his fans *and* his teammates know he'll be there when they need him.

The shots rain down and the points pile up. But Ray makes it all look easy. Bucks fans and teammates love him for his scoring touch. They are amazed by his silky steps, his swift crossover dribble and his all-around skills.

Ray plans to hear plenty of cheers in Milwaukee for many years — and silence everywhere else!

Kobe Bryant

Mr. Everything

"Kobe Bryant is my idol. I think he's the best player in the league." — Shaquille O'Neal

Coming from Shaq, an MVP and two-time champion, those are big words indeed. Many people would agree with Shaq, too. Kobe is thought of as the most multitalented player in the league. Kobe combines explosive speed, leaping ability, rock-solid defense, and a great shooting touch.

Kobe is only 24, but he is in his seventh NBA season. He jumped right from high school to the Lakers in 1996, and he hasn't stopped jumping since. Teaming up with Shaq, Kobe has turned the Lakers into the NBA's powerhouse. Los Angeles won the NBA title in both 2000 and 2001.

Kobe really proved his stellar status during the 2001–02 season when Shaq was laid low by foot injuries. The young shooting guard picked up the Lakers and carried them until the big man was back. Kobe set a career high with a 56-point game in January. On defense, he is the stopper for the Lakers, almost always facing up against the opponent's top player.

One of those players is a guy named Michael Jordan. Maybe you've heard of him? The great MJ was Kobe's hero when he was a kid. That didn't stop Kobe from showing his childhood idol a move or two. In February, he and the Lakers faced Jordan

and the Wizards. On one play, Kobe reached in, stole the ball from MJ and led a fast break to a slam. Later, he faced up and sunk a basket right in front of Michael.

In February 2002, Kobe put on a great show at the All-Star Game in Philadelphia, his hometown. He racked up 31 points against the best players in the Eastern Conference and was named the game's MVP. It was the most points scored by a player in an All-Star Game since Michael Jordan himself put up 40 in 1988.

Kobe isn't just a great player, he's a great leader. When the game gets tough, his team can count on him. Kobe proved this when he nailed game-winning shots for the Lakers in Charlotte, against the Hornets. Kobe loves to help his team win. "It's a great feeling," he said after that game.

With a future as bright as his star-spangled NBA past has been, Kobe has the chance for more great feelings in the years ahead.

Vince Carter

In-Vince-able

"Everybody in the arena — fans, coaches, both teams — knows Vince is going to take that last-second shot, and he still gets to the basket and dunks it. He just says, 'I don't care who's between me and the basket, I'm going to get there.'"
— Raptors forward Antonio Davis

It can be hard to be the player that everyone expects to win every game, make every shot and thrill every crowd. But if any player can face up to that challenge, it's Vince Carter of the Toronto Raptors.

Few players have had the soaring, above-the-rim game that Vince has. To combine

that with an outstanding outside shot seems almost unfair. He ranks among the top 20 in three-point baskets every season. He stretches defenses with his three-point range.

League-wide, Vince was one of the top 10 players in 10 major offensive categories in 2001–02. For the Raptors, he's "in-Vince-able."

That was exactly what Toronto fans expected when he joined the team in 1998. Vince won the

Rookie of the Year Award in 1999. Many have compared him to Michael Jordan. His high scoring and high flying made him a fan favorite. Three times, he has led the NBA in the All-Star voting. He also carried the Raptors to the Eastern Conference Semifinals in 2001–02.

Vince was out with an injury for part of 2002. But he was still the top vote-getter in the 2002 All-Star Game. Fans can't get enough of him! Now Vince is back at the top of his game, and hopes that this year he will lead his team to the NBA Finals!

Kevin Garnett

Life Above the Rim

"I don't think you can put any kind of price on a player's love for the game. There are so many athletes like myself that would play this game even if there was no NBA, playing on blacktop, doing what they usually do on Sunday afternoon."

— Kevin Garnett

The Minnesota Timberwolves are pretty lucky that Kevin loves basketball so much. Long-armed, high-flying, slam-dunking, KG is a good guy to have on your side. Kevin joined the Timberwolves right out of high school in 1995. Since then, he has become one of the

NBA's most dependable scorers and best all-around players.

The Timberwolves believe in teamwork. Players have to pass the ball often and work with their teammates on every play. And that's exactly what Kevin does. He has the skills to dominate a game. But he knows that teamwork is what will take Minnesota to the top.

In 1999, Kevin was joined on the Timberwolves by guard-forward Wally Szczerbiak. KG and Wally have become one of the league's most feared duos. Garnett is one of the league's leaders in rebounds. He specializes in dunks and short-range shots. Wally is a great outside shooter.

All that teamwork must be working. Led by KG, Minnesota has had one of the Western Conference's best records in the past two seasons. They have made the playoffs five times since he

joined the team. Kevin has earned five All-Star selections. And that's not all. In 2000, Kevin won an Olympic gold medal for the U.S. team!

Kevin has an amazing all-around game. He is one of only seven players *ever* to average 20 points, 10 rebounds and five assists in more than one season. That shows that he can score, help on the boards and pass almost equally well. Most players succeed at only one of these. KG uses his speed and long arms to do all three.

One of Kevin's greatest strengths is his talent for teamwork. In many games, the

Timberwolves have three or four players who score more than 10 points. KG knows he could score 30 points almost anytime he wanted to. But he also knows that that's not always the best way for his team to win. And Kevin knows that helping his team win is what really matters.

KG had to grow up fast. In 1995, he became the first high school player to join the NBA in 20 years. But he didn't let his age stop him from becoming a basketball superstar. As his teammates will tell you, he is always a great guy to have on your side.

Jason Kidd

A Passing Grade

"When Jason Kidd dreams, he doesn't dream of a big score. He dreams of the great pass."
— Nets President, Rod Thorn

You can't score in the NBA by yourself. It's that simple. Michael Jordan can't play 1-on-5. Kevin Garnett can't guard five players at once. Even Kobe Bryant needs someone to get him the ball to score. That's where passing comes in. And when it comes to passing, Jason Kidd is one of the very best there is.

Jason is a five-time All-Star. He joined the New Jersey Nets from the Phoenix

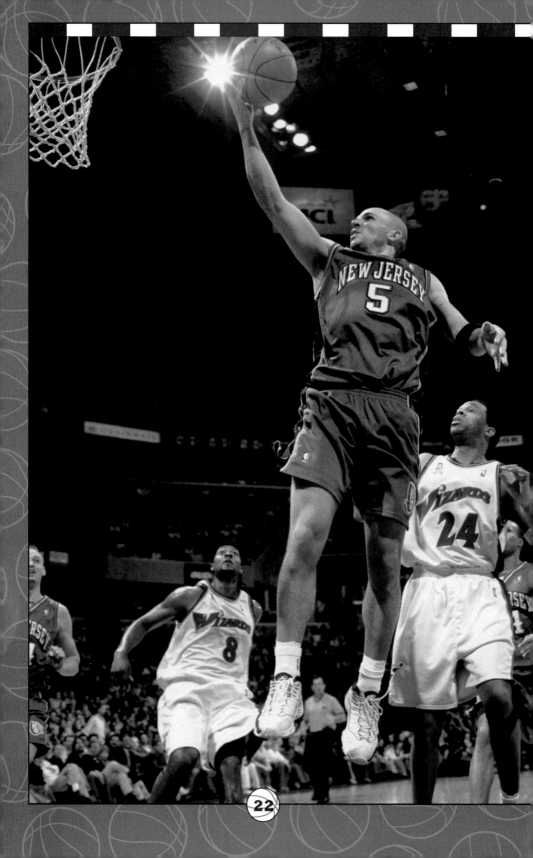

Suns before the 2001–02 season. Soon, the Nets skyrocketed to the top of the Eastern Conference. Jason didn't lead the Nets to success by scoring lots of points; he passed the ball.

Jason knows that a great pass can be just as important as a rim-rocking slam dunk. He can always get the ball where it needs to go. He floats alley-oops that hit only his teammates' hands. He finds holes in the defense just one basketball wide and puts the ball through perfectly.

Jason's teammates all know how important passing is. They often find themselves racing each other down the court on fast breaks. The winner gets the pass and the easy bucket.

"Jason finds everyone shots," says Nets guard Kerry Kittles.

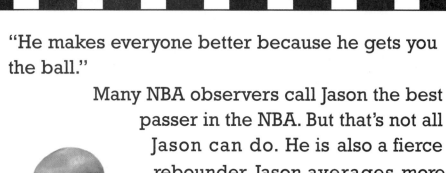

"He makes everyone better because he gets you the ball."

Many NBA observers call Jason the best passer in the NBA. But that's not all Jason can do. He is also a fierce rebounder. Jason averages more than seven rebounds a game, even though he is only 6-4.

His fast fingers come in handy on defense, too. In the 2001–02 season, Jason was one of the NBA leaders in steals.

Jason's many talents also helped him lead the league in triple-doubles, reaching double figures in points, assists and rebounds in one game. Jason's not an enormous scoring threat. He averages about 14 points per game. But he can score when he needs to — usually when no one else is open for a pass.

Sometimes one player can really make a difference for a team. He can come in and turn them into championship contenders. In 2001–02, Jason did that for the Nets, leading them to victory after victory. And he plans to do it again, for many seasons to come.

Tracy McGrady

The T-Mac Attack

"I knew he could play, but he's so much better than I thought. This kid's a star." — Grant Hill

Tracy McGrady is an NBA star, no doubt about it. He has mad moves to the hoop, can shoot with just about anybody and has become a solid defender. His nickname is "The Big Sleep," because he can take a nap anywhere. But Tracy could sleep-walk through most games and still score 25 points!

And that's not enough for this rising

superstar. Tracy works hard to improve his mind and his game.

Tracy joined the Orlando Magic for the 2000–01 season, at the same time the team got All-Star Grant Hill. But Grant hurt his ankle just a few games into the season. Suddenly, it was up to Tracy to lead his team. He didn't let his fans or his teammates down.

That season, Tracy averaged 26.3 points per game. That is the highest average ever for a player younger than 22. That was an 11-point jump from his previous season. Thanks to that incredible record, Tracy won the NBA's Most Improved Player Award. In the playoffs, he soared even higher. He averaged 33.8 points, 8.3 assists and 6.5 rebounds.

The next year, Tracy got even better. He was still one of the league's scoring leaders. Tracy was the Magic's best player by far. He led the team in both scoring and rebounding. His scoring average was almost 10 points better than any other Orlando player! Whenever the team needed a win or a big play, they turned to T-Mac. He didn't let them down. In March 2002, Tracy helped the Magic tie the Phoenix Suns in overtime. In the extra period, Tracy took charge. T-Mac scored all 10 of Orlando's points and they won the game. In another game that season, he reached 50 points for the first time in his career.

Even through the long season, Tracy works to improve his game. After every practice, he takes 200 more jump shots, most  from long range. He also tries to become a better defender. He wants to make the All-Defensive Team.

His coach is noticing his hard work. In his rookie year, some thought Tracy didn't take the game that seriously. But now Tracy works as hard as he can. And it shows.

Tracy wears No. 1 on his jersey. Maybe someday that might also be his place among all NBA players!

Dirk Nowitzki

Wunderplayer!

"I don't know how you guard Dirk. If you put a big guy on him, he faces up and shoots on him. If you put a small guy on him, he posts up or passes out of a double-team. He does it all."

— Mavericks General Manager and Coach, Don Nelson

How do you say "rebound-grabbing, slam-dunking, shot-draining 7-foot power forward" in German? Easy. Just say "Dirk Nowitzki."

The big blond from Germany is one of the top offensive players in the league. In 2001–02, Dirk was *phantastisch* (that's German for "fantastic"). He set career single-game highs in points, rebounds, field goals, free throws and three-point-ers. Soon he was one of the Dallas Mavericks' best players. The season before that, Dirk led Dallas in scoring, rebounding and assists. He was the only player other than Houston's Steve Francis to dom-inate in all three areas. In the 2000–01 playoffs, Dirk was huge. In one game against San Antonio, he racked up 30 points. In his very next game, he scored 42 points and grabbed 18 rebounds!

Dallas lost in the playoffs, but the Mavericks vowed that this season would be different. In the 2001–02 season, Dirk was awesome at both ends of the floor. He earned his first All-Star Game appearance and was selected to the 2001–02 All-NBA Second Team.

Getting better is noth-ing new for Dirk. His rebounding, scor-ing and free throw records improved in each of his first four seasons in the league. But many players score and rebound well.

Why is Dirk so special? Because he does all that at such a huge size!

Dirk is almost impossible to defend. He can throw perfect three-pointers if the players guarding him give him room. Sometimes opponents send out smaller players to double him. But then Dirk uses his passing skills to help his teammates. With his size and strength, he can own the court.

While Dallas's star Michael Finley was injured last year, Dirk had to carry the team. He didn't disappoint his teammates — or his fans! He averaged nearly 30 points per game. In four of the games, Dirk scored more than 36 points.

All Finley and the other Mavericks could say was *"Danke schoen,* Dirk, *danke schoen."* That's German for "thank you!"

Paul Pierce

The Truth Sets Boston Free

"My game is based on being an all-around game by combining fundamentals with knowledge."

— Paul Pierce

The Boston Celtics are one of the NBA's most successful and legendary teams. The men in green have won 16 NBA championships, the most ever. They have been led by many top players who combined great court skills and great leadership. Bob Cousy, Bill Russell, John Havlicek and Larry Bird are some of the most famous of these Celtics captains and stars. To that list of great players add a new name: Paul Pierce.

Paul joined Boston as a rookie out of Kansas in 1998. He quickly became "The Man" on the Celtics. Now he is one of the NBA's top players. Shaquille

O'Neal has nicknamed him "The Truth." Along his way, he has been inspired by many things.

For one, Paul knows all about the Celtics' great history. He wants to add another chapter of success. Boston fans expect success. For another, Paul entered the NBA as the 10th pick of the 1998 NBA Draft. He felt he should have been picked higher. So Paul decided to become an even better player. He had a great rookie year. His scoring averages rose in each of the next two years.

Paul's life has not always been easy. In September 2000, he was badly hurt. He had to work hard to recover. But that painful experience was just something else Paul used to improve his life.

"Everything else is small, compared to what I've been through," he says. "I just stayed strong in my mind." Paul worked hard to get better.

In 2001–02, all of Paul's hard work paid off for Boston and its fans. Paul moved into the top ranks of the NBA. He finished among NBA leaders in many offensive categories. He was third in points per game, second in three-point shots, and second in free throw percentage. He posted a career-high 48 points in a game against New Jersey in December. Thanks to Paul, Boston made it to the Eastern Conference Finals for the first time in 17 years.

At 6-6, Paul combines a beautiful jump shot with some awesome moves. He can nail a game-winning jumper from 20 feet. He can change hands in midair for a back-to-the-basket spinning-bank shot in the lane. And you'd better not foul him — he's nearly an 80 percent free throw shooter.

If he keeps this up, pretty soon he and Boston might be hanging up championship banner number 17.

Chris Webber

A King of the Court

"This is still a dream."
— Chris Webber

C hris Webber always used to dream of meeting his favorite basketball All-Stars — and now he is one! 2001–02 was Chris's ninth NBA season. He was on the best team of his career, the Sacramento Kings. The team was filled with All-Star talent from around the world. C-Webb was a big reason the Kings were among the league's most feared teams.

Many believe that the Kings play better as a unit than any other team. A big part of the reason is Chris's ability to go inside, shoot from the outside, and pass the ball. Those skills — and a burning desire to win — are what make him an NBA superstar.

Scoring has always been a big

part of Chris's game, ever since he was the 1994 NBA Rookie of the Year. He has averaged more than 20 points per game every year, except his rookie season. In each of the past three seasons, he has averaged more than 24 points per game. Chris has a lot of different shots. His best move is a baby sky-hook. He can nail it with either hand.

You want rebounding? C-Webb is the man

there, too. In five seasons, he averaged more than 10 rebounds per game.

Passing? Some call Chris the best-passing "big" man in the game. He is 6-10, but is a team leader in assists.

Defense? Chris led the Kings in steals and was among the league's top 20. He has helped shut down the league's top power forwards and centers.

What about toughness? In a game in March 2002, Chris dislocated a finger. It was a painful injury. He could have sat out the rest of the game. But C-Webb didn't want to sit down. He went back in the game and scored 22 points and grabbed 10 rebounds to help the Kings beat the 76ers. Even with an injury, he was one of the best players on the court.

C-Webb's all-around skills, combined with teammates like Mike Bibby,

Peja Stojakovic and Vlade Divac, have helped the Kings become one of the NBA's top clubs. Chris's leadership has played a big part in the Kings' rise to the top, too. He's hoping that leadership will be just enough to crown the Kings as NBA champs.

Off the Court

Stars in the Community

These NBA stars know that basketball isn't all that matters. That's why they love to help people on *and* off the court.

Ray Allen plays a big part in the NBA/WNBA youth basketball program. He serves on the Jr. NBA/Jr. WNBA Advisory Council. More than 500,000 kids take part in the program every year. He also leads the Ray of Hope Foundation that helps kids with school scholarships. Ray is a member of the NBA's All-Star Reading Team.

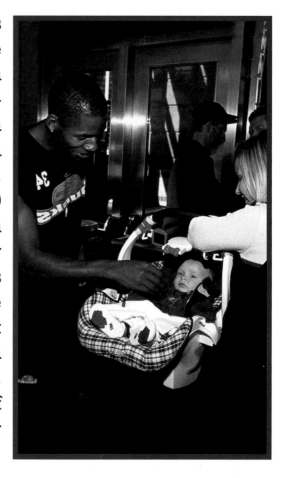

The **Kobe Bryant** Foundation raises money to help at-risk kids. One of the fun ways Kobe does this is to host the annual Kobe Bowl. Players and

celebrities show their stuff on the lanes to help a good cause. Kobe is also a member of the NBA's All-Star Reading Team.

Vince Carter makes beautiful music off the court, too. He plays the saxophone and drums. Vince sponsors Vince's Hoop Group, an organization that recognizes excellent students in the Toronto area. He is also the spokesman for the Toronto Raptors Essay Writing Contest and is a member of the NBA's All-Star Reading Team.

In February 2002, **Kevin Garnett** won the NBA Community Assist Award. He runs 4XL (For Excellence in Leadership), a group that shows kids about the world of business. Young cancer patients enjoy T-Wolves games in style in the luxury suite Kevin provides for them. He is a member of the T-Wolves All-Star Reading Team. And at a game in 2002, Kevin treated the entire arena to a free drink as thanks for cheering for the team!

The **Jason Kidd** Foundation raises money to help find cures for kids' diseases. Jason also hosts basketball camps and a golf tournament that raises money to help kids. Every Christmas, Jason

joins his wife, Joumana, to take kids from a home-less shelter out to buy toys. He is also a member of the NBA's All-Star Reading Team.

Tracy McGrady is very involved with the Orlando Magic Read to Achieve program. He also hosts his annual T-Mac bowl, which supports numerous charities in Florida. Tracy has made donations to Mount Zion Academy, where he spent one year of prep school, and Auburndale (Florida) High School.

The **Dirk Nowitzki** Foundation helps talented kids with school scholarships. The Dirk Nowitzki Basketball Academy, which is supported by the NBA and Sprite, gives all talented kids a chance to be seen by NBA scouts.

Paul Pierce and some Celtics teammates pitched in at a house in Boston. They helped fix it up for some local residents who did not have very much money.

Chris Webber has helped many charities, including the Detroit Police Athletic League. He also has his own Timeout Foundation to help kids in Washington, D.C., and also in Detroit, where he grew up. Chris has also promoted many African-American causes. He collects signed historical documents from important people such as Martin Luther King, Jr. and Frederick Douglass.